"A Gem of a Small Nabataean Temple"
Excavations at Khirbet et-Tannur in Jordan

by

Marlena Whiting and Hannah Wellman

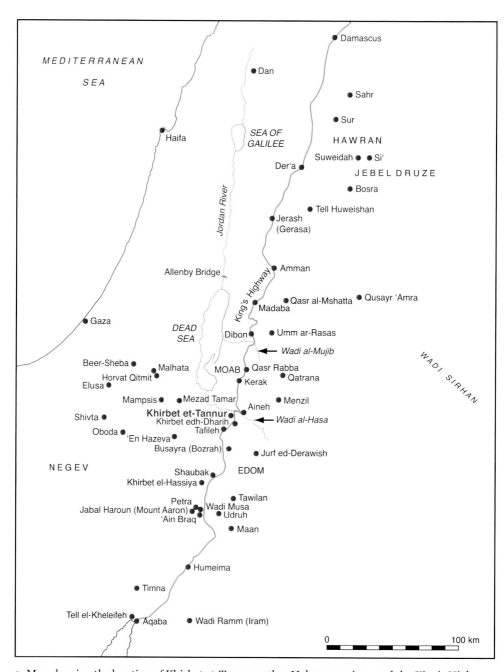

2. Map showing the location of Khirbet et-Tannur, other Nabataean sites, and the King's Highway.

3. View from Jabal et-Tannur, looking south-east, with the Wadi al-Hasa on the left and the Wadi La'abān on the right.

Introduction

The Nabataean temple complex of Khirbet et-Tannur ("ruins of the oven") stands alone at the top of Jabal ("mountain") et-Tannur in modern-day Jordan. It overlooks the junction of the fertile Wadi La'abān and the magnificent Wadi ("river bed") al-Hasa, the chasm which marks the traditional boundary between the biblical territories of Edom to the south and Moab to the north. A lonely outpost, Khirbet et-Tannur is 70 km north of the ancient city of Petra, beside the modern King's Highway, which follows the old caravan route that linked Petra to Damascus in Syria, with way stations in between. These stops included Khirbet edh-Dharih, the "mother village" of Khirbet et-Tannur, 7 km to its south.

Khirbet et-Tannur flourished over several centuries, from the 2nd century BC through to the middle of the 4th century AD. It was a thriving sanctuary, and archaeological evidence recovered from excavations shows it was an important place of pilgrimage. Worshippers paid tribute to their deities, feasted, and spent nights stargazing and celebrating the beginning of the new year at the start of spring, or the harvest later in the year.

4. Petra, the Nabataean capital, looking east along the colonnaded street to the "royal" tombs.

The Nabataeans

The Nabataeans were ancient Arabs who moved back and forth through much of Jordan and southern Syria and controlled caravan routes across the desert. Initially nomadic, they eventually established settlements such as their capital Petra in Jordan, Bosra in Syria, and their southern outpost Medain Saleh (Hegra) in Saudi Arabia. Of these, Petra is the best-known, since its buildings and monuments have served as a backdrop to Hollywood films such as *Indiana Jones and the Last Crusade* (1989), *The Mummy Returns* (2001), and *Transformers: Revenge of the Fallen* (2009).

Petra was strategically located between the Red Sea and the Mediterranean at the intersection of a vast trading network, which brought goods from Egypt, Syria, Arabia, and even India. The earliest evidence for Nabataean settlement at Petra dates to the 4th century BC. By the end of the 1st century BC, the city boasted rich architecture, rock-cut tombs, and an elaborate system for the collection and conservation of water to ensure a year-round supply. In AD 106, the prosperous Nabataean kingdom became part of the Roman Empire under the emperor Trajan. Nevertheless, although part of the wider Roman Empire, the Nabataeans still retained their own distinctive culture, reflected in their art, architecture, and language.

5-6. The Khasneh (top) and the tombs with crowsteps (bottom) show the mix of classical and Near Eastern influences at Petra.

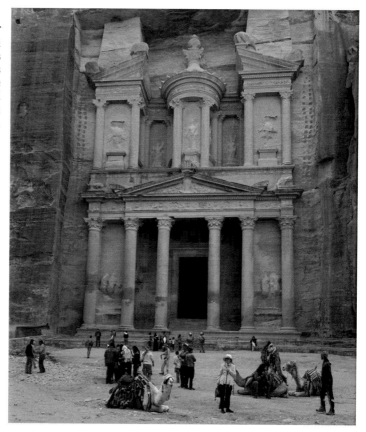

7. Nelson Glueck and Ali Abu Ghosh, 1936.

The Discovery and Excavation of Khirbet et-Tannur

Khirbet et-Tannur was excavated in 1937 by the American archaeologist Nelson Glueck (1900–1971), then director of the American School of Oriental Research in Jerusalem. Glueck was an established figure in the region, well-known for his surveys east of the Jordan River, which he carried out with his friend and colleague Ali Abu Ghosh, a guard in the Department of Antiquities of what was then called Transjordan. In 1935, surfacing of the King's Highway facilitated access into southern Transjordan, and a police station was built near Khirbet edh-Dharih. The commander of the district, 'Abdullah Rīhānī Bey, discovered the ruins atop Jabal et-Tannur and took several sculptures to his home for safekeeping. The following year, Frederick Peake, founding commander of the Arab Legion and known to the Jordanians as Peake Pasha, alerted Glueck to the discovery.

On 17 November 1936, Glueck himself examined Khirbet et-Tannur. He describes in the School newsletter how he drove from Jerusalem to Amman in Jordan at "breakneck" speed the day before, completing the 45-mile journey in two hours and fifteen minutes. That morning, he was flown from Amman to the city of Kerak, north of Khirbet et-Tannur, accompanied by Peake Pasha, who followed Glueck in his own Gipsy Moth biplane. At Kerak, they were met by the Governor, Bahajat Bey Tabbarah, who lent them a Ford station wagon to drive to the police station, where 'Abdullah Rīhānī Bey provided horses to complete the journey.

8. Peake Pasha beside his Gipsy Moth, with Bahajat Bey Tabbarah, governor of Kerak, 1936.

10. "Fish Goddess" at the house of 'Abdullah Rīhānī Bey in Tafileh, 1936.

9. Khirbet et-Tannur, cult statue of the god exposed in November 1936.

11. The team at Khirbet et-Tannur in 1937.

Glueck pronounced the sanctuary "a gem of a small Nabataean temple" and dug exploratory pits into the earth to assess the archaeological potential of the site. One of these revealed the cult statue of the god. Glueck also visited the house of 'Abdullah Rīhānī Bey in Tafileh to examine those sculptures which had been removed from the site, including the famous carving which Glueck called the "Fish Goddess" because of the fish above her head. On his return, he made arrangements to excavate the temple jointly with the Department of Antiquities of Transjordan.

The excavations spanned two campaigns totaling over eight and a half weeks in 1937: from 26 February to 16 April, and from 27 November to 11 December. The political climate west of the Jordan River was becoming increasingly violent, but despite occasional searches by local authorities of the American School's Dodge station wagon when they travelled to and from Jerusalem, Glueck and his team worked in relative safety. His immediate team included his wife Helen and, from the School, Clarence Fisher, who was a specialist in architecture, and Carl Pape, an architectural draftsman. S. J. Schweig from the Palestine Archaeological Museum was the photographer. A crew of twenty to thirty local workmen carried out the manual labour. Fisher's knowledge of classical architecture was particularly useful for the analysis of the Nabataean architectural decoration and reconstructing how the fallen blocks would have originally made up the buildings. Fisher had finished his drawings when he died in 1941, but before he could publish them and his report.

12. Excavating in front of Room 9, looking south-east.

Nelson Glueck's Archaeological Methods

Glueck himself was a pottery specialist. In the first half of the 20th century, pottery analysis had emerged as a key tool of scientific archaeology. By examining the layers or levels in which particular types of pots or ceramic vessels are found, an archaeologist is able to see variations in their appearance over the centuries. It is then possible to establish a "relative chronology" for a site, which gives the order in which different parts were built or occupied, based on what types of pottery appear in a particular period or "phase". Glueck worked out how the distinctive patterns on fine Nabataean pottery changed with time, from fine orange motifs to coarse, very dark brown ones.

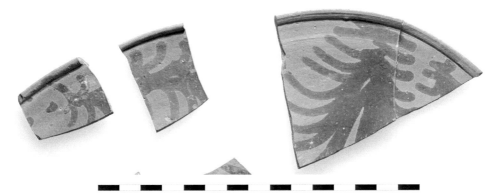

13. The most common type of sherds from Nabataean painted fine ware bowls found at Khirbet et-Tannur (HSM).

To determine a precise time or "absolute chronology" for the different phases, the archaeologist sees whether, in an assemblage of material, there are finds (such as coins) that may be reliably assigned to a fixed date. For example, if a piece of pottery is from a vessel type known to come from the 1st century AD, and it is found beneath an undisturbed floor, the floor and use of the building will date to the 1st century AD or later.

Aside from using pottery analysis, Glueck could see relative phases of construction work. He tried to date the different chronological phases at Khirbet et-Tannur by studying the construction techniques he observed in these. He distinguished different types of tooling marks on the stone blocks and noted different types of building methods and materials used in the walls. Glueck's dating of the construction phases may now be revised because of improvements in our knowledge of ancient ceramics and architecture, but his perceptiveness is still remarkable.

14. Pottery sherd from Khirbet et-Tannur labelled with its findspot by Glueck (HSM).

15. Judith McKenzie working on the records of the excavation in the Semitic Museum basement, Harvard University.

The Story of the Finds after the Excavation

In 1937, after an excavation, the custom was to divide the main objects between the host country and the excavator's institution. Some objects from Khirbet et-Tannur went to the Palestine Archaeological Museum in Jerusalem (as Transjordan lacked a museum at the time), others to the American Schools of Oriental Research (ASOR). The share in the Palestine Archaeological Museum was later transferred to the Jordan Archaeological Museum on the Amman Citadel when it was opened in 1951. Since then, some of the sculptures have been moved to the Jordan Museum in Amman for display. In 1939, Glueck shipped ASOR's share to the Cincinnati Art Museum (CAM) in Cincinnati, Ohio, Glueck's hometown in the United States.

The Second World War and the political situation in Palestine leading up to 1948 prevented full publication of the finds at the time. In 1965, Glueck published the book *Deities and Dolphins* as his final report on the temple. He examined in detail the sculptures and their relationship to the art of Petra and the Near East. He also discussed the architectural phases of Khirbet et-Tannur, for which he relied on Clarence Fisher's work. Glueck did not include a detailed discussion of the scientific finds and samples, despite having had the exceptional foresight to preserve them.

After Glueck's death in 1971, his records and the scientific samples from Khirbet et-Tannur were shipped to the Semitic Museum of Harvard University (HSM) in Cambridge, Massachusetts in the United States, at the request of Harvard Professor G. Ernest Wright, then ASOR president. This archive consisted of diaries, photographs, and bags labelled "sacks of debris". After Wright's sudden death in 1974, the boxes of this material remained unopened in the museum's storerooms until 2002, when Judith McKenzie of Oxford University visited Harvard to consult Glueck's photographs of Khirbet et-Tannur. When she and Joseph Greene, Deputy Director and Curator at the Semitic Museum, inspected the "sacks of debris", they discovered the scientific finds and samples Glueck had collected. McKenzie and a team of specialists have since analysed these unique materials using up-to-date methods and in the light of discoveries since 1937. The results of this work have developed a picture of the rituals at the site, so that the story of Khirbet et-Tannur can now be better understood.

The Site of Khirbet et-Tannur

Khirbet et-Tannur is approached via a path that snakes up the south-east slope of Jabal et-Tannur. The layout of the sanctuary is simple, consisting of three square structures, one inside the other: the Temenos or Court, with rooms along the side and a Forecourt (20.05 m wide); an Inner Temenos Enclosure (10.38 x 9.72 m); and finally, within it, the Altar Platform, which supported the main altar. We will describe the overall complex here as it was at the time of its final destruction in AD 363, before considering the different phases of construction.

16. Khirbet et-Tannur, looking south-west towards the Inner Temenos Enclosure.

Approaching the site from the east, a worshipper faced the main entrance to the Temenos. On the right was Room 10, lined with benches on three sides, with steps leading up to them. This room was a triclinium or dining room for feasting, where worshippers reclined on benches to share a meal.

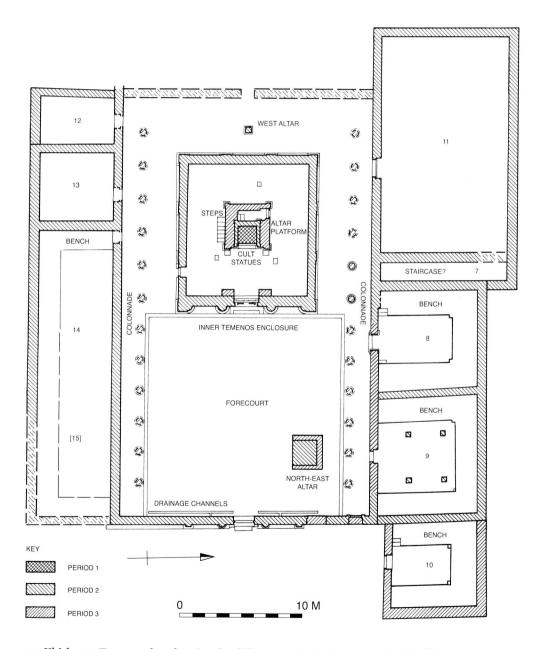

17. Khirbet et-Tannur, plan showing the different periods of construction (Judith McKenzie).

18. Forecourt, with rainwater drain on the left, looking south-west, 1937.

The Temenos (Temple Enclosure or Court)

The main doorway to the Temenos or temple enclosure was set in a facade which had columns protruding from the walls. These columns had plain Nabataean capitals on top. The doorway was decorated with pilasters with busts of deities above them: one of Tyche (the personification of Fortune) and the other of a god with a sceptre.

Passing through the main entrance to the Temenos, worshippers entered the paved Forecourt in front of the Inner Temenos Enclosure. Along the north and south sides of the Forecourt, there were rooms behind colonnades. These roofed walkways, with a row of columns in front, provided shade for worshippers. As the Forecourt was open air, its paving was carefully sloped, with a drain along the east side to allow rainwater to flow out.

On the north side of the Forecourt were two smaller rooms used for dining (Rooms 8 and 9), lined with benches. The paving of Room 8 survives and slopes down to a drainage duct in the north, so that the floor could easily be washed after use. In front of Room 9 is the surviving square base (2.45 x 2.45 m) of the North-east Altar, used for burnt animal offerings. The main room on the south side was also lined with benches for reclining diners (although called Rooms 14 and 15 by Glueck, it was probably one long room).

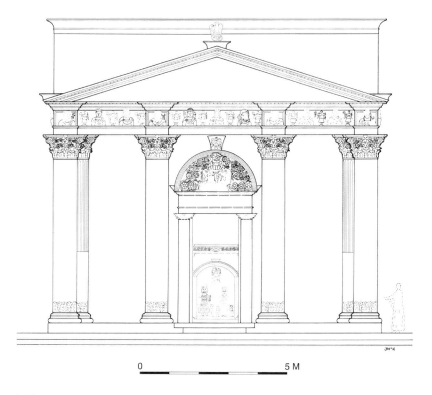

19. Khirbet et-Tannur, Inner Temenos Enclosure in Period 2, with the doors open to reveal the Altar Platform, reconstruction (Judith McKenzie).

The Inner Temenos Enclosure

West of the Forecourt is the Inner Temenos Enclosure, a tall unroofed structure with the Altar Platform in the centre. Its eastern facade was sumptuously decorated with engaged columns with floral capitals and sculptures of deities. Above the door, there was a semi-circular pediment (width 2.47 m) with the famous sculpture known as the "Vegetation Goddess" because she is veiled by leaves and framed by flowers. Above this was a triangular pediment with an eagle sculpture at its apex. The frieze below the pediment was decorated with busts of celestial deities, such as Mercury, Jupiter, Saturn, Helios (the Sun), and Luna (the

20. Khirbet et-Tannur, eagle with a snake, standing on a wreath (Cincinnati Art Museum, 1939.222).

Moon), alternating with personified representations of Victory (Nike). At either end, there was a bust of Fortune (Tyche) and a god with a thunderbolt.

Behind (west of) the Inner Temenos Enclosure, there was a medium-sized altar known as the West Altar (width 0.485 m), used for small offerings. To the south-west were two smaller rooms (Rooms 12 and 13), and to the north-west was a large room (Room 11) with a staircase leading to a second storey. Benches have not survived in these rooms, which possibly were used for purposes other than dining.

21. Bust of a god, Inner Temenos Enclosure frieze (Cincinnati Art Museum, 1939.213).

22. Helios bust, Inner Temenos Enclosure frieze (Cincinnati Art Museum, 1939.225).

23. Winged Victory (Nike), Inner Temenos Enclosure frieze (Cincinnati Art Museum, 1939.226).

24. Inner Temenos Enclosure and Altar Platform, looking south-west, 1937.

25. Front and south side of Altar Platform, with steps to the top, 1937.

The Altar Platform

The main Altar Platform was used for burnt offerings of meat and grains, and it had a niche for the cult statues built into its front. A staircase led to the top of the Altar Platform, where a sacred flame was lit and the sacrifices were burnt. Square in plan, it was constructed in three phases, each built around the last.

26. Front of the Altar Platform, during excavation in 1937.

Building Khirbet et-Tannur

The complex at Khirbet et-Tannur was developed in three main chronological periods. Each of these periods also had some sub-phases, reflecting different stages of construction or repairs.

Period 1: 2nd Century BC to 1st Century AD

The earliest objects found at Khirbet et-Tannur are two bronze coins dated to the late 3rd to early 2nd centuries BC. They were minted by Seleucid kings in the Syrian city of Antioch. In the 2nd century BC, the main altar was erected on top of a walled rubble platform. It is dated by a fragment of a bowl belonging to the 2nd century BC which was found inside. This altar was filled with burnt grain and bones from offerings made by worshippers. The altar was repaired sometime in the late 2nd or early 1st century BC. From the late 2nd century or 1st century BC through to the end of the 1st century AD, the complex was expanded to include rooms around the main courtyard, as the number of worshippers gradually grew. This upsurge in activity at the site is also reflected in the increase in the amounts of pottery from each phase.

27. Altar Platform 2, reconstruction (Judith McKenzie).

Period 2: 2nd Century AD

Sometime in the first half of the 2nd century AD, the buildings at Khirbet et-Tannur suffered some destruction, possibly caused by an earthquake that resulted in a fire, which brought down the roofs of the rooms to the north and south sides of the main courtyard. Ash deposits found in these areas show that roof timbers had burned, and the fire caused severe damage to the complex. This destruction prompted a rebuilding campaign that resulted in Period 2, the main construction phase of the site which used finely dressed, neatly carved stone blocks and sculpture on a monumental scale. In the 2nd century AD, probably during the first half, it was enlarged to include, on the east side, a niche to house the male and female cult statues and probably the sculpture of a winged Victory (Nike) supporting a ring with the signs of the zodiac.

A wall was constructed around the Altar Platform to create the Inner Temenos Enclosure. The main courtyard was paved and colonnades added along either side of it. The ornate entrance facade of the Forecourt was also erected. Rooms were built behind the colonnades, some with benches on three sides for dining. A dining room (Room 10) was also added outside the east end of the main courtyard. Other altars, such as the North-east and West Altars, were added.

Period 3: 3rd Century to mid-4th Century AD

In the late 2nd or early 3rd century AD, an earthquake damaged the temple complex. Consequently, the colonnade around the main Court was replaced. The niche for the cult statues in the Altar Platform was surrounded by elaborate decoration that included floral and vegetal reliefs, a frieze of grape vines, and, most importantly, busts of figures representing the signs of the zodiac on the pilasters at the corners. Originally twelve busts in total, the heads have been knocked off many of them. Only the bottom two busts have survived intact: the "Fish Goddess", now known to be the personification of Pisces, and the "Grain Goddess", now known to be Virgo. These are more stylised in appearance than the sculptures of Period 2.

After another earthquake, repairs to the stairs show that the Altar Platform was still in use at this time. Room 14, a bench-lined room to the south of the main courtyard, also continued to be used.

An exceptionally strong earthquake on 19 May in AD 363 had a final devastating effect. Centred in Galilee and felt as far away as Petra and Jerusalem, it also caused a fire at Khirbet et-Tannur that substantially damaged the complex. The facade of the Inner Temenos Enclosure collapsed onto the paving below. The complex was never rebuilt. Worship mostly ceased, although overnight visitors may have continued to travel to the site in the 5th and 6th centuries AD, since a few cooking pots and lamps that date to these centuries have been found. Unlike some temples and high places, Khirbet et-Tannur was not later re-developed as a Christian or Islamic place of worship.

28. Virgo ("Grain Goddess") and joining block, Altar Platform 3 (Cincinnati Art Museum, 1939.227).

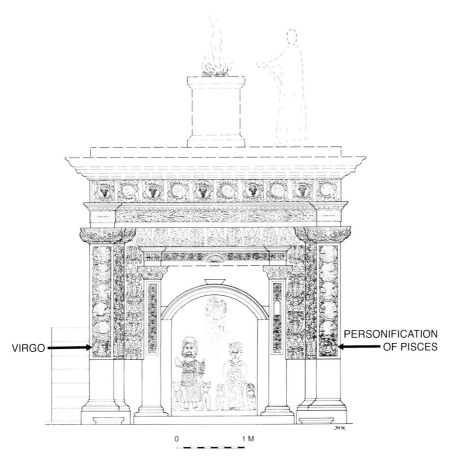

VIRGO ⟶

⟵ PERSONIFICATION
OF PISCES

0   1 M

29. Khirbet et-Tannur, Altar Platform 3, reconstruction showing position of busts of Virgo (fig. 28) and the personification of Pisces (below) (Judith McKenzie).

30a-b. Personification of Pisces, Altar Platform 3 (Jordan Museum, Amman), h. 0.27 m.

Khirbet edh-Dharih:
"Mother" Village of Khirbet et-Tannur

Khirbet et-Tannur was not a place of permanent settlement, since it lacked a perennial water supply. The closest source of water was a cistern located on the mountain, some 35 m below the temple, which was filled by runoff. Instead, the religious complex was a destination for pilgrims.

Many worshippers would have stayed at the village of Khirbet edh-Dharih, 7 km south of Khirbet et-Tannur and the third caravan stop from Petra on the King's Highway to Damascus. Khirbet edh-Dharih had a year-round water supply from three nearby springs. These include ʿAin ("spring") al-Laʿabān which is mentioned in an inscription found at Khirbet et-Tannur, showing that this name has survived for two thousand years. The springs supported cultivation and habitation. In antiquity, the village consisted of roughly twenty houses, a villa, a temple, and pilgrimage facilities, which included a bathhouse and caravanserai where visitors could be lodged. Khirbet edh-Dharih was excavated by a French-Jordanian team in the late 1980s to 2000s, providing information unavailable in Glueck's time.

The links between Khirbet edh-Dharih and Khirbet et-Tannur are reflected in their archaeology. Nabataean construction at both sites was often begun and developed simultaneously. At Khirbet edh-Dharih, the first version of the temple, constructed in the 1st century AD, was 15 by 15 m square, complete with an altar. A bathhouse and caravanserai were also erected then.

31. Khirbet edh-Dharih in spring.

32. Khirbet edh-Dharih temple, looking towards its facade and interior.

A new, larger version of the temple was built about AD 100–150, coinciding with the main (Period 2) construction at Khirbet et-Tannur. The temple at Khirbet edh-Dharih was incorporated into a large religious complex, with a colonnaded forecourt, followed by yet another forecourt at the southernmost limit of the complex. Comparison between building styles and sculpture of the temples at Khirbet edh-Dharih and Khirbet et-Tannur shows that the same workmen contributed to both sites during the first half of the 2nd century AD (Period 2 of Khirbet et-Tannur). Additions to Khirbet edh-Dharih around AD 200 coincide roughly with construction at Khirbet et-Tannur during Period 3.

Although the temples at these two sites have very different plans, indicating different functions, a relationship between them is suggested by the busts of male personifications of the signs of the zodiac on the main frieze of the temple at Khirbet edh-Dharih, alternating with Nikes. These busts are in the equivalent position to those of the celestial deities on the facade of the Inner Temenos Enclosure at Khirbet et-Tannur. Because the French excavators recognised that signs of the zodiac were part of the architectural decoration at Khirbet edh-Dharih, the "Fish Goddess" and "Grain Goddess" at Khirbet et-Tannur could be seen for what they were: representations of Pisces and Virgo, as explained below.

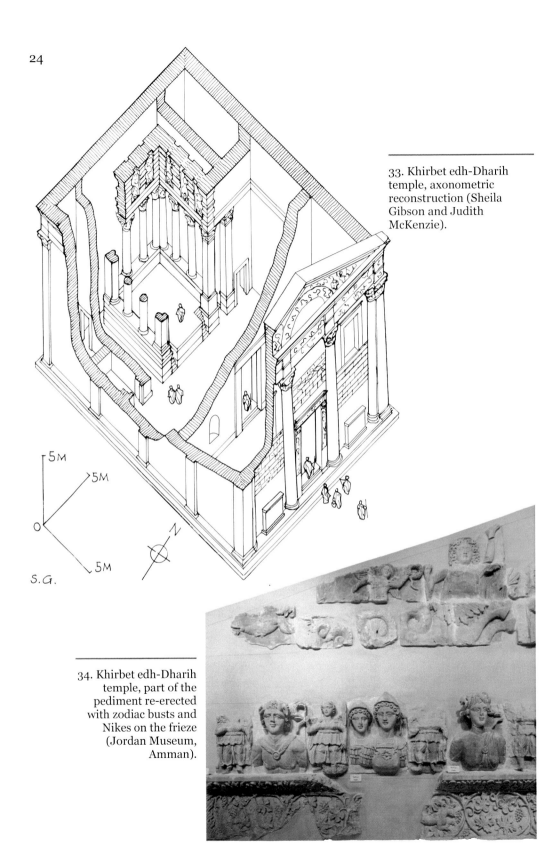

33. Khirbet edh-Dharih temple, axonometric reconstruction (Sheila Gibson and Judith McKenzie).

34. Khirbet edh-Dharih temple, part of the pediment re-erected with zodiac busts and Nikes on the frieze (Jordan Museum, Amman).

35. Khirbet edh-Dharih temple, zodiac busts (Taurus – the bull, Gemini – the Twins, and Cancer – the Crab) and Nikes on the frieze (Jordan Museum, Amman).

The colonnaded forecourt at Khirbet edh-Dharih had associated dining rooms, and the southern court also had three dining rooms built, in ca. AD 200. The southern portion was in use until the earthquake of AD 363, after which the Khirbet edh-Dharih temple complex was abandoned for over a century. However, as the temple there had not suffered as much damage as the one at Khirbet et-Tannur, it was refitted as a church in the 6th century. Another earthquake in the 8th century AD toppled part of the facade, and finally, an earthquake in the 18th century caused the remainder of the temple to collapse.

Nabataean Religion

One of the main obstacles to our understanding of ancient Nabataean religion is the lack of contemporary written accounts describing their beliefs, mythology, or rituals. The passages in classical authors (Greek and Latin) had sometimes become confused because of mistakes when their texts were copied over the centuries. The Greek geographer Strabo (born ca. 64 BC), in his *Geography* (16. 4. 26), mentions that the Nabataeans worshipped the sun from the tops of their houses. Strabo is probably referring to the roofs of temples with staircases leading up to them. At Khirbet et-Tannur, the top of the Altar Platform would have served a similar purpose, with a staircase leading to it.

Most of what we do know about Nabataean religion comes from inscriptions mentioning particular gods and goddesses, and from what we can infer from temple architecture. Khirbet et-Tannur is a major source of our knowledge because the earthquake of AD 363 destroyed a working sanctuary, preserving the remains of ritual offerings and sacrifices. As this type of evidence has not survived at any other Nabataean temple, Khirbet et-Tannur provides a unique glimpse of religious practice there. Other temples were frequently reused, even if by "squatters". In addition, dry conditions at the top of Jabal et-Tannur also helped preserve material.

36. Petra, stone block representing Isis, with her symbol at the top.

Representations of Nabataean Deities

Early in their history, the Nabataeans worshipped simple stone blocks which served as non-figurative or "aniconic" representations of their deities. These blocks are often found in niches carved into a cliff face, although a few are free-standing. Sometimes these blocks were given anthropomorphic features, such as square eyes or a stylized nose.

With the expansion of trading networks and the resultant wider contact with and exposure to other cultures, the Nabataeans adopted the practice of representing their deities in human form. Over a hundred fragments from figured

sculptures were found at Khirbet et-Tannur. Originally, they would have been bright-
ly painted. Most of this sculpture was carved in Period 2, in the first half of the 2nd
century AD.

To represent their deities in figured form, the Nabataeans used a sculptur-
al vocabulary drawn from nearby cultures, as we will see. Thus, the cult statues at
Khirbet et-Tannur show the influence of the Near Eastern, Egyptian, and Graeco-Roman
artistic traditions. But this does not mean that the image of a Nabataean divinity
should be equated automatically with a particular foreign deity. Nabataean sculptors
simply borrowed the attributes of deities whom they recognised as having powers
comparable to those of their own gods. Thus, for their own supreme god and goddess,
they adopted features of supreme deities of other cultures. Furthermore, these figural
al representations did not supplant the aniconic tradition, which continued into the
Islamic period. Rather, they were additional to it. Some foreign gods, however, were
worshipped in their own right. For example, Isis, the Egyptian goddess of fertility who
was popular throughout the Mediterranean, was worshipped at Petra.

The Edomite Storm God Qos

The only god identified by name
at Khirbet et-Tannur is Qos, mentioned in an inscription carved on
a plain stone pillar or stele (height
0.40 m), found near the Altar Platform. Qos was a storm god of the
Edomites, the Iron Age predecessors
of the Nabataeans mentioned in the
Bible. As a weather god, Qos is anal-
ogous to Dushara, supreme deity of
the Nabataeans with authority over
the sky, storms, and fertility. Since
the inscription mentioning Qos at
Khirbet et-Tannur is written in a
Nabataean script dating to the 1st
century BC, it provides evidence for
continuity of religious practice from
the Edomite period (10th to 6th centuries BC) into Nabataean times. The
name Qos was also used at Bosra, in
southern Syria, as late as the 2nd
and 3rd centuries AD.

37. Khirbet et-Tannur, Qos stele (Cincinnati Art
Museum, 1939.268), h. 0.40 m.

38. Khirbet et-Tannur, cult statue of the god (Cincinnati Art Museum, 1939.224), h. 1.15 m, w. 0.57 m.

Cult Statue of the God

Artistically, the statue of the god at Khirbet et-Tannur combines features of the supreme gods of nearby cultures: Greek Zeus (Jupiter in the Roman pantheon), Syrian Hadad, and Egyptian Serapis. The figure wears a classical dress with a cloak over a type of Greek tunic called a chiton, and his beard and hair show distinct classical influence. He resembles Zeus or Jupiter and holds a thunderbolt in his left hand to produce rain, and a sceptre in his right to symbolise his authority. Around his neck is a Near Eastern twisted neck-ornament, called a torque, with a lion's head decoration at each end. Like the Syrian god Hadad, the god of Khirbet et-Tannur is flanked by bull calves and holds a thunderbolt. But like the Egyptian god Serapis, he had a bushel of wheat balanced on his head, although it is now damaged. Thus, the artistic presentation suggests this god has power over the weather and the abundance produced by its rain. The male cult statue might represent the Nabataean supreme god Dushara.

39. Hadrian's Villa at Tivoli, Italy, statue of Zeus.

40. Theadelphia (Batn Ihrit), Egypt, statue of Serapis.

41. Dura-Europos, Syria, relief of Hadad and Atargatis (Yale University Art Gallery).

42. Dura-Europos, Syria, relief of Hadad.

The Female Cult Statue

Nabataean religion involved the dualistic pairing of a male divinity with a female consort. Of the goddess's cult statue, only part of the lion throne (height ca. 0.40 m) and her foot survive. Dushara's female counterpart was Allat, often associated with the Greek goddess Athena. Allat also was represented with a lion on either side of her throne to emphasise her role as mother and protector. Allat was worshipped over a wide geographic range. At Petra, however, the goddess al-'Uzza, associated with Aphrodite or Venus in her planetary role, instead is mentioned as Dushara's consort. Perhaps Allat and al-'Uzza were two names for one supreme goddess.

Glueck had thought that the female statue represented Atargatis, the supreme Syrian goddess. She too was shown on a lion throne, often beside her male counterpart Hadad. But Atargatis is not known to have been worshipped by the Nabataeans, and many goddesses are seen flanked by lions, including the Anatolian Cybele and the Mesopotamian Ishtar. The Nabataeans may therefore have adopted this aspect of Atargatis to represent their own goddess.

44. Palmyra, Allat on altar of Malkou.

43. Khirbet et-Tannur, lion and foot from cult statue of goddess, Period 2 (Cincinnati Art Museum, 1939.218a, 218b, 278, 287), h. ca. 0.40 m.

45. Palmyra, fragment of a copy of the archaic cult statue of Allat.

The Vegetation Goddess

The so-called Vegetation Goddess panel was positioned above the main doorway of the Inner Temenos Enclosure which led to the Altar Platform. She is shown with flowing hair and veiled in leaves framed by florals. The flowing hair, leaves, and flowers represent the life-giving effects of water. The prominent location of this carving at the entrance to the Inner Temenos Enclosure suggests that the worship of a water or fertility goddess was an important part of ritual at the sanctuary.

Glueck thought that the Vegetation Goddess was another representation of the Syrian fertility goddess Atargatis. However, in classical art, leaves on the faces of deities usually indicate that they are water deities. Thus, she probably is a personification of the nearby spring of La'abān which irrigates the groves near Khirbet edh-Dharih. An inscription at Khirbet et-Tannur dating to 8/7 BC mentions building works dedicated by the guardian of this spring. The prominence of the Vegetation Goddess at the sanctuary may be related to this guardianship, even though that inscription is over a century earlier in date than the sculpture.

46. Khirbet et-Tannur, Vegetation Goddess (Jordan Museum, Amman).

The Zodiac

One of the most famous discoveries from Khirbet et-Tannur is the magnificent sculpture of a ring showing symbols of the zodiac encircling a bust of the Fortune goddess, Tyche. A winged Victory (Nike) holds aloft the zodiac ring (0.36 m in diameter).

47. Khirbet et-Tannur, zodiac Tyche (Cincinnati Art Museum, 1939.233 and Jordan Museum, Amman).

The statue is now in two fragments. Glueck excavated the upper fragment with the zodiac, which is now in the Cincinnati Art Museum, Ohio. Later, the lower fragment with the Nike came to light. It is displayed in the Jordan Museum in Amman. The feet of the Nike have never been found, but they were probably represented as standing on a globe. The sculpture dates from the first half of the 2nd century AD, when it was carved in Period 2, along with the cult statues and the busts on the Inner Temenos Enclosure facade.

The goddess in the centre of the zodiac, Tyche, is identified by her "mural crown" showing city walls and towers, because she was believed to preside over the fortunes of cities. She wears a veil over her crown. Behind her right shoulder is a crescent moon. Over her left shoulder is an unknown object that resembles two sticks bundled together, one topped with a crescent moon, the other with an ear of wheat or a pine cone. These symbols represent Tyche's associations with the heavens and fertility. There are two other busts of Tyche at the site with this object, which seems to be unique to the Tyche of Khirbet et-Tannur.

At Khirbet et-Tannur, the zodiac signs are represented by a combination of human busts and animal figures, each about 0.10 m high. Aries (the Ram) and Capricorn (the Goat) are represented by human busts, rather than the conventional animals. The two fish representing Pisces face the same direction, pointing to the influence of Egyptian art, in which this arrangement is typical. The fish usually face opposite directions in Roman zodiacs.

Some of the zodiac signs have raised dots carved onto the fields behind them. It was first thought that these dots represented positions of planets in the relevant part of the night sky represented by the zodiac sign, and that these could potentially indicate the precise date when the zodiac was carved. But they do not seem to correspond to any known alignment of the planets, and so their purpose remains a mystery.

48. Khirbet et-Tannur, bust of Tyche, from Forecourt entrance, with unique symbol behind her right shoulder, as on the zodiac Tyche (Amman).

49. Khirbet et-Tannur, zodiac Tyche, upper block (Cincinnati Art Museum, 1939.233).

The order in which the twelve signs of the zodiac are arranged is significant. In zodiac rings found elsewhere (for example, Rome), the signs are placed sequentially, running either clockwise or counter-clockwise in a full circle. At Khirbet et-Tannur, the signs were not meant to be read in a continuous circle. Instead, the ring is made up of two halves: Aries through Virgo (March/April – September/October) run down the left-hand side of the ring, with Libra through Pisces (October/November – February/ March) down the right-hand side.

Thus, the zodiac ring reflects a division of the year into two halves. The Nabataeans followed the Babylonian calendar and so considered the spring equinox in March to signal the beginning of a new year. Since the spring equinox occurs within Aries, that sign is placed at the top of the half of the ring representing the months of spring and summer. The autumnal equinox falls within Libra, which therefore appears at the top of the other half of the ring, which represents the autumn and winter months.

This organisation of the zodiac is reflected in the busts of female deities that were added to both sides of the cult statue niche in Period 3. The lowest two busts

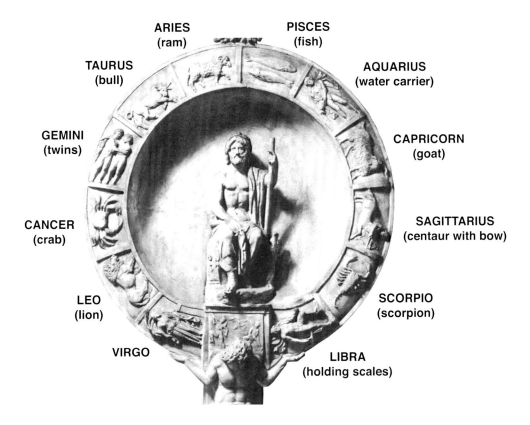

50. Rome, zodiac ring, supported by Atlas, with Zeus/Jupiter in the centre.

have survived with their heads intact. The busts, which Glueck called the "Grain God-dess" and "Fish Goddess", are now known to be personifications of Virgo and Pisces respectively. The placement of the "Grain Goddess" and "Fish Goddess" at the bottom on the left and right, respectively, corresponds to the organisation of the zodiac-ring. As viewers faced the cult statues, they would see, along the left-hand side, from top to bottom, the busts of Aries through Virgo. On the right-hand side, from top to bottom, were the busts of Libra through Pisces.

Because the sanctuary at Khirbet et-Tannur is aligned along an east-west axis, the rays of the rising sun on both the spring (vernal) and autumnal equinoxes would strike the niche in the Altar Platform which housed the cult statues. Consequently, it is suggested that the zodiac might have been placed between the statues, a little above them, where it would have been illuminated by the dawn light on the first day of the new year at the vernal (spring) equinox. At the dawn of the autumnal equinox, the sun would again illuminate the cult statues and the zodiac. On these major solar events, Khirbet et-Tannur would have seen an influx of pilgrims.

51. Khirbet et-Tannur, upper part of small statue of goddess (Jordan Museum, Amman), h. 0.40 m.

52. Khirbet et-Tannur, small statue of goddess, showing side of her crown with Isis symbol (Jordan Museum, Amman).

53. Khirbet et-Tannur, fragments of a Period 3 cult statue of the god (Cincinnati Art Museum, 1939.235, 262, 282, 284).

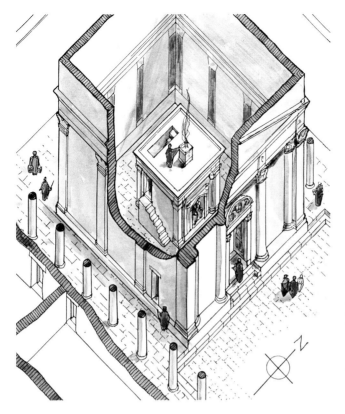

54. Khirbet
et-Tannur,
reconstruction of
Inner Temenos
Enclosure and
Altar Platform
(Sheila Gibson).

Other Sculpture

Busts of planetary and celestial deities are prominent on the frieze of the Inner Temenos Enclosure at Khirbet et-Tannur, where Helios, Jupiter, Saturn, Mercury, and
the Moon can be identified as part of a series. Emblems of the sun and moon (like the
crescent moon behind the Tyche in the centre of the zodiac ring or the Helios crown
on the figure appearing on the circular altar) affirm the importance that astrology and
astronomy had for worshippers at the site. They are accompanied by symbols of rain
(thunderbolts) and the fertility it brought (floral vines).

Other statues, though smaller than the main cult statues, would have also
played a significant role in local ritual. In the Inner Temenos Enclosure, for example,
Glueck and his team found the top half of a sculpture of a seated female figure. It may
be a miniature of the female cult statue, and the detail of its carving dates it to Period
2. Her dress is Greek in style, and she has a Near Eastern style torque, similar to the
one seen on the male cult statue. Her hair is unveiled, and she wears a crown decorated with the symbol of the Egyptian goddess Isis repeated around it, rather than being
used alone at the front as was the usual convention. Pieces identified as belonging to
an additional male cult statue, carved in Period 3 (height of head 0.21 m), were also
found in the Inner Temenos Enclosure. As with the smaller female figure, it is not
clear where it originally stood.

Worshipping the Gods

After the final destruction at Khirbet et-Tannur, the buildings were abandoned and not disturbed, re-used, or rebuilt. Consequently, the evidence was preserved from when it was still in use, making it possible for archaeologists to better understand Nabataean religious practices when the site was a focus of ancient worship.

Fortunately, Glueck's archaeological methods were in advance of his time. Many excavators of the late 19th or early 20th century simply focused on the recovery of beautiful objects and the reconstruction of grand buildings, with little attention paid to their archaeological contexts. In the first half of the 20th century, archaeologists began to record and study the pottery found in excavations more systematically. Glueck himself kept meticulous records and carefully gathered for scientific analysis not only pottery, but also samples of bones, plants, glass, and metal which the dry conditions at the top of Jabal et-Tannur had helped to preserve.

As advanced as Glueck's methodology was, his excavations still pre-dated the development of tests that archaeologists use regularly today. In addition, in his day, there was not much material excavated at other Nabataean sites against which he could compare his finds. But because of Glueck's foresight, it has now been possible to study his material using up-to-date methods and take into account more recent discoveries providing vital comparanda.

Lamps and Night-Time Ritual

Lamps were necessary for worship at night, when the stars and some planets would be visible. At Khirbet et-Tannur, interest in the night sky was suggested by the zodiac and the busts of celestial deities. Lamps may have been used to light the way for processions to the sanctuary. The dates of the lamps found there range from the beginning of the 2nd century AD to the 6th century AD.

Glueck found not only the usual single-wick lamps, but also fragments from two types of lamps specifically designed to create much more light: "socket and saucer" lamps and polycandela. The "socket and saucer" lamp has a thick wick and so would have had a bright flame. The polycandela were multi-tiered with rings of nozzles on several levels and would have shone like candelabra. At Khirbet et-Tannur, fragments of nozzles were found which would have come from polycandela, like a more complete example from Petra. The floodlights of antiquity, they enabled a variety of night-time activities to take place. We can imagine worshippers staying up at the site through the night to watch the sky and the morning sunrise, especially on the vernal (spring) or autumnal equinox.

55. Khirbet et-Tannur, wheelmade round lamp (HSM).

56a-b. Khirbet et-Tannur, slipper lamps.

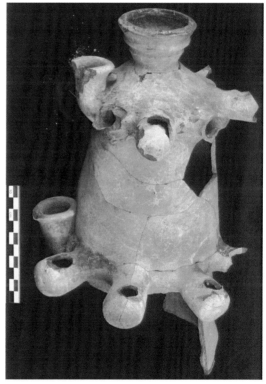

57a-b. Khirbet et-Tannur, socket and saucer lamp (Amman) and fragment (HSM).

58. Petra, near Qasr el-Bint temple, multi-tiered polycandelon.

Incense

Two small incense altars were placed on either side of the niche in the Altar Platform that contained the cult statues. One is inscribed with the name Alexander Amrou ("Alexander, son of 'Amr"), who had dedicated it. This altar is decorated on the front with a male figure holding a sceptre and a thunderbolt, as well as with a figure of Nike on each panel to the side. The names "Alexander" and " 'Amr" are Greek and Semitic respectively, showing the cultural mix of the Nabataeans and reflecting local and Graeco-Roman influences. The second altar was roughly circular in shape. Sculpted on the surviving fragment of it, there is a winged Victory (Nike) and a figure holding torches who is attired in the Greek dress of a woman, but wearing the crown of the Greek sun-god Helios.

59. Alexander Amrou altar with traces of burnt incense (Jordan Museum, Amman), h. 0.55 m; w. 0.31 m.

60. Circular altar, left-hand panel, with figure holding torches (Cincinnati Art Museum, 1939.212).

Scattered around the site were other smaller, free-standing altars, each unique in appearance. These small altars were used for burning incense as an offering. As the incense burnt, the smoke was thought to carry prayers up to the gods. The size of these altars makes them readily portable, as they range in height from 3.5 to 23 cm. They were probably carried up to the temple by individual worshippers, who, after making an offering, would leave these altars behind as personal dedications to the gods. Charred remains of incense were also found on the altar of Alexander Amrou in front of the cult statue niche of the Altar Platform. Glueck had these analysed, confirming that they were the remains of incense.

62. Incense altar shaped like an Ionic capital (Cincinnati Art Museum, 1939.232).

61. Incense altar dedicated by Mati''el (Cincinnati Art Museum, 1939.228).

63. Deep basin incense altar (Cincinnati Art Museum, 1939.279).

Animal Sacrifice

In addition to incense, offerings of sacrificed animals were also made. Although a few of these animals were chickens, most of the animal remains found came from sheep and goats, but notably also cattle. The animals appear to have been sacrificed when young. The absence of toe bones tells us that they were butchered off-site. The charred animal bones and burnt grains from the main altar dated to Period 1. These bones had been burnt at high temperatures, indicating they were intended as offerings, rather than just being cooked.

64. Burnt bones, from inside the Altar Platform (HSM).

The number of bones of goats found was greater than the number from sheep, perhaps reflecting a similar ratio in local herds that were the likely sources for the animals. Because the bones of cattle – calves especially – are rare at other Nabataean domestic sites, their appearance at Khirbet et-Tannur suggests that they were sacrificed for ritual purposes. The cattle bones were only found in

65. Unburnt bones, from west offertory box (HSM).

the main altar, and it is notable that young bull calves are depicted on either side of the cult statue of the god. The North-east Altar is a similar size to the Period 2 main altar, suggesting that it was used for similar sacrifices. The West Altar was probably used for smaller sacrifices, possibly chickens.

Bones which had not been burnt were also recovered from Khirbet et-Tannur. These were found in "offertory boxes" in the paving of the Inner Temenos Enclosure. Each box had a stone lid to ensure the safety of the offerings. Two were located on either side of the main altar, with the third directly behind it.

Grain and Offering Cakes

The charcoal collected from the site came from trees such as acacia and tamarix. Priests or pilgrims appear to have gathered this wood on their way to the site to fuel the fire for the sacrifices and for cooking the meat to eat in the dining rooms. Although Jabal et-Tannur today lacks vegetation, the wadis at the base of the mountain support shrubs and trees.

Grain played a large role in ritual worship at Khirbet et-Tannur. Emblems of agricultural abundance, such as representations of wheat, appear throughout the site. Burnt grains were found alongside animal bones in the earliest altar of Period 1. There was also a layer of burnt grain under the paving slabs of the Inner Temenos Enclosure. It is possible that the grain was a deliberate ritual offering placed under the paving slabs as part of the construction carried out in Period 2. Charred grains of wheat were also found behind the male cult statue on the Altar Platform.

These grains included cereals such as emmer wheat, barley, and perhaps durum. Emmer wheat was the predominant type. It was found in quantities up to three times greater than other types, such as durum. This proportion is the reverse of what is normally found in domestic archaeological contexts of the period in Jordan, indicating that emmer wheat was deliberately chosen for religious purposes. The grains deposited at the site were carefully prepared. The wheat was picked extremely clean. Great care had been taken to present a fine, finished product to the deities.

One of the most surprising discoveries was the identification of charred fragments of burnt offering cakes found in amongst the burnt grains. These cakes were made from flour and water. The additional presence of charcoal and charred grains in the offering boxes suggests that the grains and cakes were ritually burnt inside the boxes. The bones may have been stored inside afterwards.

66. Charred emmer wheat, from Inner Temenos Enclosure (HSM).

67. Pieces of burnt offering cakes (HSM).

68a-b. North-east offertory box, before and after opening in 1937.

Dining Rooms for Ritual Feasting

Foodstuffs were not just the preserve of the gods. The prominent positioning of dining rooms around the Forecourt reflects the importance of feasting as a cultic activity. Diners would have reclined on benches in the different dining rooms. The various types of ceramics and glass objects found in these rooms confirm this. The temple complex at Khirbet edh-Dharih and some complexes at Petra also included dining rooms.

69. Room 8 with benches around three sides, looking north, 1937.

Crockery and Cooking Pots

Dishes used for the feasting and preparation of meals and sacrifices were made of pottery. Bowls, goblets, beakers, cups, bottles, storage vessels, and cooking pots have all been recovered from the site.

There is now a larger body of ceramic material against which to compare the pottery from Khirbet et-Tannur in order to establish their dates. Glueck had established a chronological sequence for the typological development of Nabataean ceramics, but subsequent discoveries at other sites have meant that his system can be refined. The dates of the ceramics are important because they indicate when activities occurred. Analysis of the pottery has shown the gradual growth in religious activity at the site, with an increase during the 1st century AD, leading up to the main Period 2 construction in the first half of the 2nd century AD. The earliest pottery belongs to the 2nd century BC.

70. Khirbet et-Tannur, jug and cooking pots photographed for Glueck (Amman).

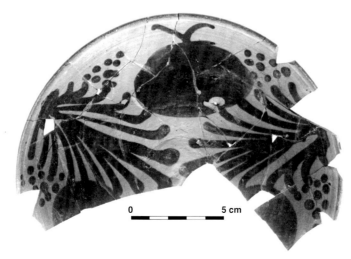

71. Khirbet et-Tannur, fragments of painted Nabataean fine ware bowl (Amman).

Glass

The glass vessels from Khirbet et-Tannur consist of bowls, beakers, and flasks. Some may have been used as drinking vessels during the ritual feasts. The medium-sized flasks may also have been used as oil containers. The bowls may have held small amounts of food for either the gods or the diners themselves.

Scientific analysis has provided information about the sources from which the glass was made. Much of the glass from Khirbet et-Tannur seems to have been produced from different sources along the coast of the Levant and then recycled nearby, probably at Khirbet edh-Dharih, where worshippers and pilgrims could have bought the vessels on their way to Jabal et-Tannur. This glass is chemically different from glass found at Petra, which has less evidence of recycling, possibly because it might have had, as a major city, more sources of fresh glass. This difference also suggests that glass was not transported from Petra to Khirbet et-Tannur.

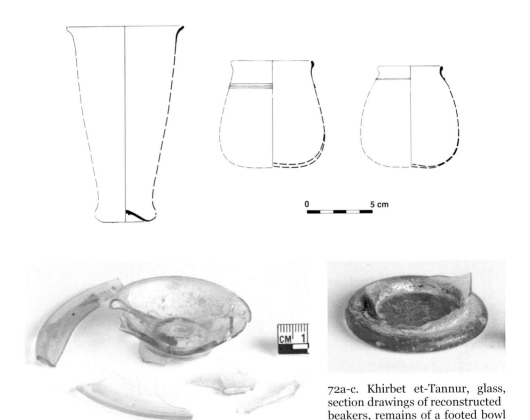

72a-c. Khirbet et-Tannur, glass, section drawings of reconstructed beakers, remains of a footed bowl and of a flask (HSM).

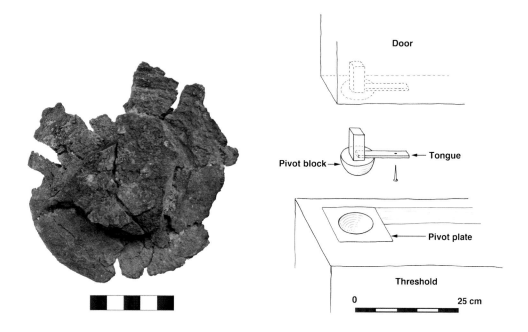

73. Door hinge of ultra-high carbon steel, top view (HSM).

74. Hypothetical reconstruction of door hinge.

Ultra-high Carbon Steel

One of the most interesting discoveries made using scientific methods was the identification of ultra-high carbon steel, later used for swords, such as Damascene blades.

An iron door hinge found in the door frame socket, with the charred remains of the doors at the entrance of the Inner Temenos Enclosure, was so badly corroded that there seemed no original metallic iron left in it. This was inconsistent with conditions at the site, however, which is very dry and should preserve iron well. A thin section was subjected to x-ray examination and microscopic study, which showed that the metal for the door hinge was ultra-high carbon steel.

Because ultra-high carbon steel is exceptionally hard, it is useful for objects that experience a lot of wear or need to have a very sharp blade, but it is also difficult to shape. It had been generally assumed that it was not frequently produced in the Nabataean region until the 6th century AD (in the Hauran). The metal analysis for the door hinge at Khirbet et-Tannur, however, suggests that ultra-high carbon steel might have been more extensively used in the Near East between the mid-2nd century and the mid-4th century AD than once thought. This remarkable discovery is one example of the new light which scientific analysis can shed on the ancient world.

Conclusion

Glueck's work at Khirbet et-Tannur and the research by McKenzie and her team have revealed the archaeological importance of this "gem of a small Nabataean temple". The rich architecture, sculpture, and archaeological remains paint a dazzling picture of a vibrant pilgrimage site, where the supreme Nabataean god and goddess were worshipped, ensuring seasonal rains and agricultural abundance through the deities and planets which controlled the weather. The complex existed solely for worship and ritual practice. It was an important regional sanctuary whose significance to the Nabataeans – and possibly the Edomites before them – must have been profound. By climbing to the top of Jabal et-Tannur, worshippers were brought into the presence of their gods and exposed to the full wonder of nature and the open sky.

A comparison may be made to the modern Bedouin tradition of pilgrimage to "Aaron's Tomb", a mountain-top shrine on Jabal Haroun, outside Petra, where the biblical prophet Aaron is traditionally thought to have been buried. The Palestinian ethnographer and medical doctor Tawfik Canaan (1882–1964) noted that, twice a year, in February and again in the summer, worshippers would visit there, and some would spend the night. He described the burning of incense and the sacrificing of animals. The meat was cooked and divided between the poor and the person making the offering. The archaeological evidence suggests that similar rituals took place at Khirbet et-Tannur.

Further Reading

Augé, C. and Dentzer, J.-M., *Petra: The Rose-Red City* (London: 2000).
 Pocket-book which provides a short introduction to the city of Petra.
Glueck, N., *Deities and Dolphins* (London, 1965).
 Glueck intended this book to serve as his final report on Khirbet et-Tannur.
Healey, J. F., *The Religion of the Nabataeans: A Conspectus*. (Leiden, 2001).
 Examines the different types of evidence for Nabataean religion.
Markoe, G., ed., *Petra Rediscovered, Lost City of the Nabataeans* (New York, 2003).
 Useful chapters: F. Villeneuve and Z. Al-Muheisen, "Dharih and Tannur: Sanctuaries of Central Nabataea" (pp. 83–100); and J. S. McKenzie, "Carvings in the Desert: The Sculpture of Petra and Khirbet et-Tannur" (pp. 169–95).
McKenzie, J. S., *The Architecture of Petra* (Oxford, 1990).
 Detailed study of the classical facades and monumental buildings at Petra; also discusses the relationship between Petra, the architecture of Alexandria, and wall-painting in Roman Pompeii.